Search:
Do I Really Need SEO?

The Enterprise-Level Playbook to Grow Your Brand
with Search Engine Optimization

© 2025 EWR Digital

Written By Matthew Bertram

MatthewBertram.com

Paperback ISBN: 9798866434022

SEARCH

DO I REALLY NEED SEO?

The Enterprise-Level Playbook
To Grow Your Brand
With Search Engine Optimization

MATTHEW BERTRAM

"Matt's approach to business has always impressed me! He seems to always know just what his clients need and how to get them to that next level. He takes the complicated process of SEO and makes it relatable for anyone that wants to grow their business online."
— Debbie Papp, CPA/Owner, The Window Center

"Since working with EWR Digital, the client's SEO rankings have been consistently improving. What's most impressive about the team is their in-depth knowledge of the industry. Both sides communicate regularly via phone calls and email."
— Peter Germanese, President, Venture Loop

"EWR Digital is incredible to work with. They partner with you and help you define your strategic vision. They sit down with you, help you design what messages to send to your potential and your existing customers. They're incredibly flexible, have great ideas, and bring a lot to the table. I felt like I had a partner in this entire process."
— Kathleen Lines, Critter Control

Preface: Why You're Invisible (And What It's Costing You)

Most businesses aren't losing to better products. They're losing to brands that know how to show up when it matters most—in search.

When a prospect Googles a problem you solve, do they find you?

Or do they land on your competitor's blog, an industry leader's site, or a company no one's even heard of—yet?

Search is the starting point for nearly every buying decision. Whether it's a parent exploring after-school programs, a CEO vetting vendors, or someone checking if golf carts are street legal, search determines who gets the click. And whoever gets the click, gets the client.

Right now, brands just like yours are quietly building trust at scale. Not with flashy ads, but through strategic search visibility. They're dominating results, generating traffic around the clock, and becoming the go-to names in their space.

This isn't magic. It's SEO.

But not the outdated kind full of jargon and shortcuts.

This is a strategic, enterprise-ready framework for growing your brand through search, built on E-E-A-T, powered by AI, and designed to turn visibility into measurable revenue.

Introduction

What are people saying about you and your organization?

More importantly, what's Google saying?

Staying top of mind today means staying top of search. Your ideal customers, investors, journalists, and even future employees are all searching for signals of relevance and trust. If you're not showing up — someone else is.

Think about the last time you needed a quick answer, a tax rule, a legal detail, a recipe, a kid's program. You found content from H&R Block, a law firm, Betty Crocker not by accident, but by design.

These organizations aren't just chasing traffic. They're playing the long game of influence. They've built an SEO machine, one that turns simple content into serious visibility.

This playbook shows you how to do the same.

You'll learn why search is still the #1 driver of digital trust, how to build compounding visibility over time, and what it takes to turn your website into a growth engine — not a digital brochure. No gimmicks. No fluff. Just the strategic SEO mindset that Fortune 100s and high-growth firms are using right now to stay top of market.

Top Of Mind

Search engine optimization isn't just about rankings. It's about *relevance*. It's about making sure your brand is visible the moment your ideal customer starts looking and staying top of mind when it matters most.

Think of SEO like digital public relations. You wouldn't expect a one-off press release to build lasting influence. Real PR involves research, planning, outreach, follow-ups, experimentation, metrics, and long-term relationship building.

Now apply that same mindset to your SEO.

Just like PR includes **paid, owned,** and **earned** media, great SEO does too.

- Paid media may get you quick traffic, but the moment you stop paying, it's gone.

- Owned media like your content, and your site builds the foundation.

- Earned media such as mentions, backlinks, and featured content builds trust and credibility in the eyes of both people and search engines.

SEO is the system that unites all of it and drives growth that compounds over time.

But here's the catch: **most businesses are doing SEO wrong.**

They hire a digital agency, get a few generic blog posts and technical tweaks, maybe a monthly PDF report full of confusing charts… but no real clarity. No keyword gains. No pipeline impact.

Here's the truth:

Great SEO is not a checklist. It's an ecosystem.

To succeed, you need a strategy built by people who understand content, code, data, and human behavior and how they all work together. You need alignment between writers, developers, analysts, and strategists. It's not just about rankings — it's about **revenue**.

If you've tried SEO before and felt underwhelmed, you're not alone. Ask yourself:

- Did the agency track real business outcomes or just vanity metrics?

- Did they explain what they were doing and why, or was it all hidden behind buzzwords and black-box tactics?

- Were your campaigns truly customized or just cookie-cutter?

- And most importantly… was your bottom line growing?

Chances are, what you tried wasn't SEO, at least not at the level that works today.

Because real SEO is **living, breathing strategy**. It evolves with algorithms. It adapts to changing customer behavior. It requires constant iteration, innovation, and cross-disciplinary expertise.

Post-COVID, the digital landscape is more competitive than ever. Every brand is online. Every business is trying to get found. The difference?

The winners are the ones who *engineer visibility*, not hope for it.

Paid Ads?

What about online advertising agencies that will run paid ads for you? Google Ads, YouTube Ads, Facebook Ads, Bing Ads, media buys? Seems set-it-and-forget-it, in theory, right? What may disappoint you is that this process involves burning through cash for months. Creating many new ads several times per day, never mind refining your existing ads that are already running. Trying out different landing page copy.

The dirty little secret in the affiliate advertising world is that this is much harder than you think to do effectively despite what they say and requires an entire system. Most landing page funnels, at best, only break even.

In other words, there's more to paid ads than "set it and forget it." Your (in-house or outsourced) team will have to put in constant time and money on ads that probably lose you money on the frontend, and after you have spent your ad budget, or those ads stop converting, the traffic stops. All of that can work out for your company, but that is the strategy you may not be considering.

Google has over 200+ ranking factors, which change constantly. Some SEO's believe that Google intentionally adds many organic search ranking rules to get you to "give up" and simply run ads to get traffic. However, if you simply run ads and neglect optimizing your website (as we'll explain in this book), then you will still have trouble competing. If you decide to run ads, implementing good SEO will enhance those results. Also, by focusing on organic SEO, you have an opportunity to be more strategic and cost-effective with retargeting ads.

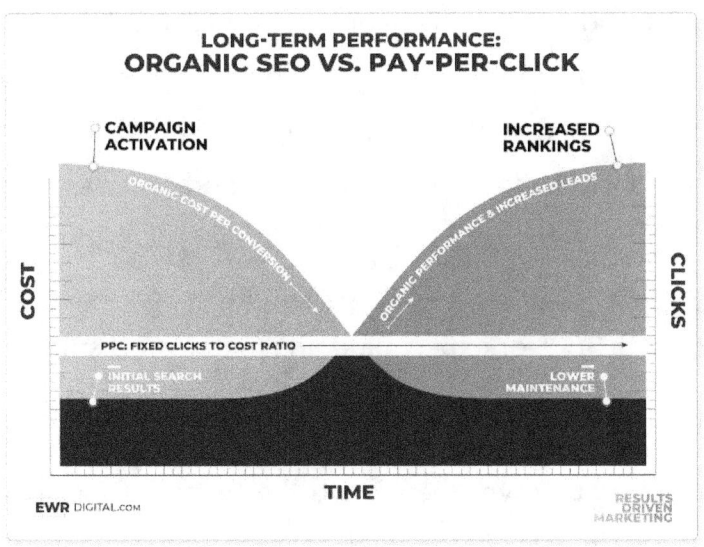

Another reason your focus should be on organic search and not on ads: paid visitors are desperate buyers, or coupon seekers. Remember that time you had to get "that" software solution quickly? Intending to refund all but one later, you installed five apps and purchased five software programs, with a limited amount of time to try out each, just because you wanted to solve a specific short-term problem. Also consider a prospect looking at an organic (free) search result of yours next to a (paid) advertisement.

You can't avoid the "search" aspect of your business, but it is hard to do at scale, especially if your team is not used to constantly chasing knowledge (the latest

SEO trends), numbers (your own metrics), labor (the work, time, and energy to constantly create and rebuild), and strategy (the big picture, high level decisions, adding to the system, and throwing out what doesn't work). It takes a special type of thinking and motivation. This is why many agencies don't focus on SEO, or expect paid ads to deliver results.

What's the solution for you, specifically? Do what you can on your own, then leave the heavy lifting to an expert, like EWR Digital. When you contact an attorney, accountant, or decorator, you don't approach empty-handed. You probably have many scanned documents, notes, ideas, and questions, even if you realize you have blind spots and you "don't know what you don't know." In this same sense, do you what you can with what you know, then come to us to tell us what your "starting point" is.

KPIs

What are your Key Performance Indicators and what are you currently measuring? Which conversions on your site would you like to optimize? Many people think about conversions on their front page, but what about getting people to keep coming back to your app or platform?

For fun, think about what sort of conversions an enterprise like Airbnb would be looking to optimize. They would want new visitors to sign up, but they would also want sellers and buyers logging in regularly, using their app and waking up through notifications. Airbnb would want their auto-generated emails (customized to each user) to have high click-through rates. They would want to minimize abandoned carts or at least follow up on them.

Are you happy with the videos on your site and what they accomplish? Would you like to perform new experiments on your content and copy? Are you on a fast web host, and even if you are, do your pages load extremely fast, every time? (You should check your Core Web Vitals in Google Search Console.) Does your web presence, search rankings, and landing pages all match with the rest of your public relations efforts?

I would like to help you to take your enterprise SEO (search engine optimization) efforts more seriously and deliberately, so you can enjoy bigger, better, and measurable results. Sure, every enterprise-level organization has heard of SEO, but many are not consistent in their efforts or take it seriously at all levels of the organization. Most people outside the Marketing department have trouble caring about SEO.

A pro tip: if apathy is something that you are dealing with is instead of trying to explain to the IT department and leadership on why they need to improve marketing, frame it as a "bug" and submit it as a ticket. *"This programing error of the website content, how it's built, or the lack of links to the site causes us to lose traffic and millions of dollars of revenue to our competitors!"* That perhaps will get their attention.

It's time to get back to basics to properly (and consistently) implement SEO for your business in the following areas:

- **technical SEO:** "checking all the boxes" so that your website is crawled and indexed (registered in Google Webmaster Console, site map generated and submitted, a fast-loading and mobile friendly website).

- **on-page optimization:** fixing up your own web pages in areas like title tags, URL structure, headings, content, and internal links to make them user-friendly for humans and easily understood by search engines.

- **content strategy and development:** look at your existing content, edit what you have, and create new content (keyword research) that is valuable, informative, and engaging.

- **link building:** acquiring high-quality backlinks from other websites.

- **local SEO:** attract customers, prospects and visitors from specific geographic areas and directories to drive foot traffic to your business.

- **analytics and reporting:** tracking, measuring, analyzing and reporting search traffic, keyword rankings, backlinks, conversion rates, and user engagement metrics.

- **improved user experience:** create a website that is easy to navigate, mobile responsive, and provides engaging/relevant content.

All of this totals up to long term results for your organization. The benefits continue for months or years, unlike paid ads or "hoping for the best." You get top of mind awareness. You seem to be everywhere. You are showing up for keywords at all steps of the buying process. Attention, Interest, Decision, Action (AIDA). Your website, your organization, your solution, will be familiar to your ideal prospects when they are ready to make a buying decision you will be favored and become their first choice without them realizing it.

Frequently Asked Questions

1. What are you doing to remain in the news, stay relevant, and continue to be a thought leader in your space?

2. What are 5 quick questions I might research about your organization? Have you typed these into search engines? How long does it take to find a quick answer?

3. What's one public relations task you can think of, that your organization performed in the past 12 months?

4. What do you think is your current weakness or missed opportunity when it comes to your search engine rankings, results, and traffic?

Search by Matthew Bertram

Chapter 1: High-Level Search Engine Optimization | Experience, Expertise, Authoritativeness And Trust

Let's talk about getting your organization to make the most of its website traffic. Meaning, you want a lot of "ideal" prospects to come to your site, and you want to funnel them to the correct destination on your site.

... So your progress with search engine optimization falls into one of these possibilities:

1. You're doing nothing.
2. You're still filling the basic **foundational** holes (making sure your content is indexed, monitoring backlinks or ranking, improving your website's loading speed), or:
3. You're iterating on an ongoing basis to improve your website's **ranking factors** and

user experience. You know how your pages rank, for which keywords, and how you are rising in the ranks. You know your numbers like website visitors for specific pages, time spent on page, conversion rate, and the funnels (paths) visitors take on your website. You are modifying your website's menu navigation and front page. Or:

4. You have the foundation and your **metrics** in place and you're pursuing the cutting edge. When a search engine like Google changes their algorithm, their guidelines, or you just pick up some tips or best practices, you're in an excellent position to roll out changes in your website.

No matter your level of progress, search engine optimization is never complete. There's also a correct and incorrect approach to take regarding your website. The "wrong" way is to use black hat tactics, shortcuts, cheats, and hacks. What short term results will that get you and for how long? I believe it makes more sense for you to pursue the search engine optimization fundamentals that may be lacking in your organization or are not receiving enough ongoing attention.

The Buyer Journey

With all the cliches about low user attention span and crowded competition, it actually makes sense! Pre-internet, if you were searching for back pain remedies, you might visit your local bookstore or public library, browse through a card catalog, possibly have them request a book from another location, and you would return a week later to pick up that book, written years or decades ago, to find your answer.

As an exercise, let's pretend that during the early days of the internet, you were searching for a professional, like a lawyer or therapist. What were your options? Flip through the Yellow Pages or call your town's Chamber of Commerce. If you were lucky, perhaps you'd hear an ad on the radio, see a park bench billboard, or get a recommendation from a friend. Incredibly unreliable and inefficient marketing that is fractured, not focused!

You see, the quest of search engines like Google is to index the entire planet and organize this information in a usable way. The "collective world's knowledge" or the "human hive mind." If you ask a question, even an incomplete one, its goal is to provide exactly the right answer. Let's say you simply searched the phrase "Boy Scouts of America" and nothing else. Google should be helpful enough to provide the answers you want, even though you haven't specified whether you're looking up information about the Boy Scouts organization, a specific event or activity, or just searching for a local troop near you. Google is trying to figure out your intent.

You could be asking about this on a smart speaker, in which case you're waiting for the device to transcribe your spoken words, find your answers, and speak them back to you. You are already impatient. Or perhaps you're typing this question on a mobile device, on a small screen and keyboard, multitasking. Even when you land on a website, you expect to find your answer within just a few seconds and a couple of taps on the screen. This monumental task of the Search Engines is to predict the answer you are looking for and retrieve it for you as quickly as possible.

Get Rewarded Every Step Of The Way

To get your head wrapped around a helpful SEO mindset and strategy, let's pretend you were an enterprise SaaS providing a point-of-sale solution for self-storage locations. If a customer at a self-storage facility wanted to rent a new unit, update their billing information, or print a key card, they would use one of your internet-connected databases.

You can already imagine the sorts of questions a prospective buyer would have, what they would search, which search results they could click on, which pages of your website they would click, and where you would like that buyer to end up.

What do you need to have in place for Google to reward you every step of the way?

First, what **keywords** do you rank for? Too many business owners are short-sighted and want to rank at the top of page one for a short, almost-impossible, non-specific keyword phrase on a particular topic or theme that their ideal buyer or prospect would not type in a search box, these are called "head terms." As mentioned earlier, the head terms are important to rank in the directory for but you do not have to be first page and it may be too competitive now. You want to go after the long tail key phrases.

In those "early" days, Google wanted you to provide your own keywords (through meta keywords but this was abused by marketers and the search engines don't rely on what you tell them now, they crawl your page to decide what keywords (keyphrases) are appropriate, but the idea is similar: you want to publish content (web pages) targeting specific keywords that are closer to the bottom of the funnel where there is specific intent.

Second, how high in the **rankings** do those keywords rank? Google's original algorithm looked at how often a human searched for a phrase and clicked a search listing. If someone searched "self-storage kiosk Houston" and clicked your link near the bottom of page two, Google would typically reward this by moving your listing up in the ranking, further up that page and eventually to page one. These days, Google looks at a lot more ranking factors. For example, they will show you different search results based on your location and search history. But the idea is the same: target many relevant keywords with lots of helpful content.

Also, did you know that the majority of traffic is congregated in the top 3 search results? This means that you have the best result for a given term or phase that someone is searching for. You want to find the long tail non-competitive terms if you are going to win long term.

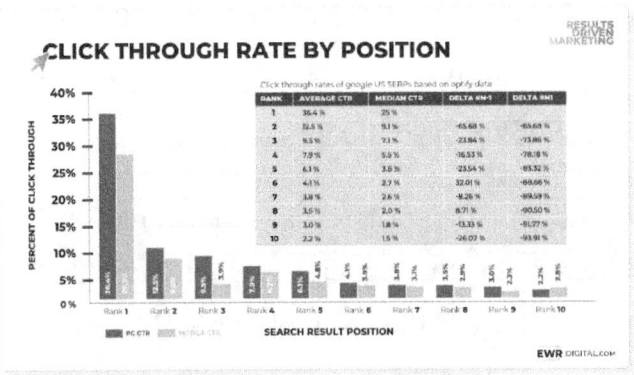

Third, who **links** to your web pages?

Imagine if you published a guest article in Forbes Magazine which linked back to your site. If appropriate, are you listed on local sites like Yelp? Is your organization setup on social media sites? In the old days, Google would rank you higher if "good neighborhoods of sites" linked to you, and punish you if "bad neighborhoods" linked in or that you linked to them. Does every website you are associated with (through links or other websites they are associated with) follow Google Guidelines?

Just as with the rest of Google's algorithm, it's not so simple anymore, but consider what it would be like to dominate the search results. What if someone searched for a relevant keyword, and the first two pages of results were filled not just with web pages you own, but review sites, news articles, and the like... all linking back to you?

Then, when someone clicks that link onto your website, what is that experience like? Does this visitor quickly find what they're looking for? Does that web page load in less than two seconds, with optimized (compressed) images? Does your website's navigation make sense? Does your site look okay on a mobile

24

device? Does your website look well-established and legitimate... meaning it has an SSL certificate, legal and terms of use pages, and relevant contact information? Have you made your web pages easy to crawl via Google Search Console and XML sitemaps?

It's too easy to fall into the trap of sticking with outdated or just flat wrong search engine optimization advice, like "keyword stuffing" or buying a bunch of spammy backlinks or blowing minor factors out of proportion and trying to over optimize for them— it looks unnatural to Google and they penalize you for the very thing you want to rank for. Trying to "cheat" or outsmart an algorithm that can change monthly and is getting smarter every day, doesn't work. Proceeding without a plan also doesn't work. Instead, give Google what it wants (helpful content that provides the appropriate answer) while also acting strategically in pursuit of your goals like keyword dominance, link building, and a fast website.

YMYL and EEAT

Let's jump into two important concepts that you'll need to keep top-of-mind in your quest to give the search engine algos what they want.

The first is **YMYL: Your Money or Your Life.** Google calls these "pages or topics that could potentially impact a person's future happiness, health, financial stability, or safety." Consider what misinformation could alter someone's life when it comes to current events, government (laws that have passed or are about to pass), financial news (the stock market), health (natural remedies), or shopping (for example, a car you are about to buy).

You don't have to use a lot of your imagination to understand how an unethical internet marketer could create a ton of pages, articles, videos, and content on different social platforms and blogging sites, link them together, and rank them quickly— pushing affiliate links, trashing one company's reputation, or artificially elevating another product.

Google categorizes YMYL content to a stricter standard and gives more weight in terms of **EEAT:**

Experience, Expertise, Authoritativeness, and Trustworthiness. What do you need to keep in mind to hit these four targets?

Experience: what first-hand life experience do you have about this topic? For example, if your blog post or video reviews a product, do you show the product and is it clear you have used it?

Expertise: are you a subject-matter expert? Do you have the proper knowledge, credentials, and qualifications to teach this information? What information are you sharing publicly that the search engines can find?

Authoritativeness: what is your reputation in your industry? Are you seen as a thought leader? Do you link to external content to prove your claims, and do others link to you that are also considered experts in your space?

Trustworthiness: how reliable and transparent is your website itself? Is the website HTTPS secure? Do you have a privacy policy, contact form, and is it clear who owns and runs the site?

Google wants you to create content that is original, helpful, and "written by people, for people." If someone is harmed by your information, who can they contact? Is it clear who your company is and who your authors are— do they have bios and social media information? Does your company conduct keyword research and content audits? Do you moderate and control your user-generated content? Do you monitor your reviews and backlinks?

Core Web Vitals: LCP, CLS, FID

Search engines like Google want you to fix your site for user experience and speed. Does everything make sense when someone lands on your web page, and does it load quickly?

Google has codified some of these user experience needs into three metrics called Core Web Vitals. When you optimize your site to meet these three Core Web Vitals, Google will reward you with a higher ranking. Core Web Vitals involves...

- **LCP or Largest Contentful Paint (loading):** how long does it take for the largest content element (image, video, or text) to become visible within the user's viewport? Try to make this happen within 2.5 seconds.

- **CLS or Cumulative Layout Shift (visual stability):** if your elements shift as the page loads, this can be frustrating for users clicking. Minimize words and elements that shift around on the page as it loads. The more these elements shift, the higher your "CLS score" becomes, so you must keep your CLS score below 0.1.

- **FID or First Input Delay (interactivity):** when a user interacts with your webpage (clicking a button or link), how much of a delay is there until the browser's response to that interaction? Keep this to 0.1 seconds (100 milliseconds) or less. Many times, this issue is caused by loading large JavaScript libraries, broken, uncached, or uncompressed (un-minified) JavaScript/CSS. Some tools use the very similar metric **TBT or Total Blocking Time** to measure how long it takes for your page to become fully interactive.

You can check these Core Web Vitals using tools we'll discuss later such as Google Search Console and Google Lighthouse.

Your eyes may have just glazed over— that is okay. There are technical components of the search and website user experience, and you may need an expert to help.

Other web vitals to pursue: site speed (some tools refer to this as a Speed Index), a mobile friendly site, safe browsing (privacy policies, Content Security Policy headers to prevent Cross Site Scripting), HTTPS ("https://" in your URL and a padlock icon), no intrusive interstitials or malicious redirects.

The more you dive deep into search engine optimization high-level strategy (as opposed to the overly technical side) you'll notice the same best practices appearing: Google wants you to have a fast-loading site, free of errors and problems, that search engines can understand (i.e. sitemaps, schema, headings), that helps your human visitor find the correct information.

Web Accessibility: POUR

Your website should be designed and developed in a way that is usable and navigable by people with disabilities— this includes visual, auditory, cognitive, and motor impairments. Did you know that only 13 percent of people find that they don't generally experience accessibility issues when shopping online? Did you also know that people with disabilities shop online nearly twice as often as the general population?

"Accessibility" also covers temporary impairments like a user with a broken arm, or someone recovering from surgery. There are also situational impairments covering a visitor who may be on public transportation or otherwise on a limited internet connection— all the more reason for a fast loading, optimized page. What if your visitor is in a brightly lit room such as presenting on a stage— does your site need a "Dark Mode" option? Perhaps they are unable to play loud audio and you should provide captions or a transcript of video/audio content.

You can easily get lost diving into the legalese within the 1990 Americans Disability Act, 2010 UK Equality Act, or 2019 European Accessibility Act, but the bottom line is that you should target the four principles of accessibility: Perceivable, Operable, Understandable, Robust...

- **Perceivable:** is your site accessible to screen readers? Do you provide text alternatives including alt tags for images? Do videos have captions, and do audios have transcripts? Can someone read the text even if CSS styles are disabled?

- **Operable:** is the page functional and usable, regardless of the device someone uses, perhaps a mobile device with a small screen? Can someone use your site even if they do not have a mouse to navigate?

- **Understandable:** can your visitor clearly understand what you present in your interface, with predictable and consistent navigation? Is the site at an appropriately targeted reading level, with consistent font styles and a logical navigation structure?

- **Robust:** does your site function across as many outdated, current, and future devices, operating systems, and browsers? Consider an elderly visitor who may not understand how to switch browsers, or may be using outdated equipment.

To examine your current accessibility level and begin to make improvements, you can optimize your page titles, headings, anchor text, breadcrumb links (navigating back to or top-level content), alt text, and sitemaps. By the way, this also helps your search engine results positions (SERPS).

A logical starting point to tackle your accessibility problem is Google Lighthouse. Like many SEO tools, it will analyze your website and provide a score so you can see how your site speed, required HTML tags and attributes, images, links, CSS, and JavaScript measure up. It will identify specific issues and give you advice on solving them.

These questions might seem overwhelming at first, but they are all important components of your SEO strategy. Keep iterating through these goals. Take inventory of what you have already established and consider what you are lacking. You may need to do some deep-thinking and revisit these ideas again and again. Let's start with the low-hanging fruit— your existing web pages.

Questions to Consider

1. What can you do in the next 30 days to judge your existing content for E-E-A-T (Experience, Expertise, Authoritativeness, and Trustworthiness)?

2. How heavily does your organization and your webpages relate to YMYL (Your Money or Your Life) content? Are you a "clear YMYL" topic (i.e. evacuation routes, prescription drug details), "may be YMYL" (weather forecasts), or "unlikely YMYL" (entertainment news)?

3. Can you identify 5 search keywords to focus on, either those you rank for, or want to rank for?

4. What high traffic sites are linking to you? Can you identify five prominent backlinks to your site or some you might be able to get?

Chapter 2: On-Page SEO | Content, Technical Optimization, Keywords, Conversion

You want search engines to understand and rank your page. Even if you know very little about search engine optimization, you have probably done a lot of things right, just by virtue of hosting with a decent cloud-based web host and using a popular content platform (i.e. WordPress)... but there's definitely room for improvement, especially since your competitors are working constantly to outrank and outperform you. Also, if you are using other platforms, you can still rank. The reason most people use WordPress is because there is a special relationship between Google and WordPress.

What do you need to know and where should you improve? Let's break this problem down into more manageable pieces. First, the overall strategy:

- **Keyword research and optimization:** relevant, high-traffic keywords in your content, headings, title tags, meta descriptions, and URL structure
- **Content quality:** valuable and engaging content that aligns with your user's intent... does it solve their problem and relate to the journey that brought them to your site and this specific page?
- **User experience (UX):** readable fonts, content organized in a way that makes sense, navigation that is intuitive
- **Internal linking:** improve navigation by linking related pages together... encourage your website visitors to continue engaging with your content

Then, specific measurable factors:

- **Title tag:** accurately describe your content and use the correct keywords
- **Meta description:** make users want to click into your web page from the search results
- **Heading H1, H2, H3 tags:** highlight key points within your web pages for easier readability,

and make it easy for a visitor to jump to a specific section of your page

- **URL structure:** ensure your page URLs themselves are descriptive and contain relevant keywords
- **Image optimization and Image Rich Search:** make sure the filename of your images themselves make sense, and that those images have alt tags so that robots understand what your images are about (First image is most important so use your target keyword in the title or Alt so you can rank for image results on search engines as well)
- **Page loading speed:** minimize file size where possible— especially images, that can be compressed "just right" and be in a compact file size and still look great, enable caching so your site delivers web pages at lightning speeds, and optimize code ("minify" or compress included JavaScript libraries)
- **Mobile friendliness:** do your webpages look great across different devices— phones and tablets with both large and small screens? We've all seen web pages where the text looks too small on a phone, or an image is way too

large on a tablet. Have you recently loaded your website on a different device?

- **Schema markup:** if you haven't already, look into the relevant structured data that applies to your web pages. For example, a web page may include information about a specific author, or in an e-commerce context, there may be schemas about a product's price, ratings, and reviews.

Try searching Google for any recipe and you'll see the cooking time for that recipe shown right in the search results. Ask any smart speaker for the ingredient list of any recipe and it will read them off to you. How is this possible? The schema markup, that is invisible to a human webpage visitor but read and indexed by search engines! Google has a Structured Data Markup Helper tool to help you with this. This is also important in local SEO, and is overall one of the most underutilized tools.

Spend some time on Schema.org and you will be surprised what types of schema you might be able to add to your website to help the search engines better understand what it's about.

Artificial Intelligence (AI)

Artificial intelligence has and will play a huge role in search engine optimization. You have already been using artificial intelligence for many years in the form of Netflix suggestions, Amazon recommendations, and the speech recognition on your phone.

It's easy to forget that just a few years ago, finding an answer to a problem from a web search was time consuming. It was slow, awkward, and many times, you wouldn't even find your answer— or you may have had to click on search result after search result. You now get your answers much faster. The reason is that search engines like Google are using artificial intelligence to better rank (and better display) search results.

How can you use this knowledge about artificial intelligence to boost your organization's SEO efforts? There are tools like SurferSEO, SemRush, Ahrefs, SE Ranking, Spyfu, Clearscope, MarketMuse, and BrightEdge that can look at your existing content. These tools can recommend changes to better rank for keywords, ideas for more helpful content you can create, how to better structure your content, and find backlink opportunities.

ChatGPT

ChatGPT (Chat Generative Pre-trained Transformer) is a LLM (Large Language Model) chatbot that replies to a prompt you provide. It will help you generate (and revise) content, plus work on your keyword strategy.

You can use ChatGPT to create product descriptions, blog posts (entire articles), and social media posts. It can translate, proofread, grade, structure your content, generate meta descriptions, reply to customer reviews, create personalized responses to customers based on chat history and past purchases, and write marketing emails.

When ChatGPT became mainstream, SEO agencies everywhere feared that Google would identify and de-rank AI content, rendering it useless in many ways. However, we were surprised when Google announced their stance: AI-generated content is okay, if it is useful. However, you should add your own opinion and use real life examples to help prevent it from being de-indexed. You need to know that the standard of great content is now being taken to the next level if you want to rank in those top spots.

The most important aspect about ChatGPT is in prompt engineering. If you ask, "Write me an article about Plumbing or Kitchen Remodeling" you will get a decent attempt at a blog post, but that prompt does not give the chatbot enough information to create what you specifically imagined or enough to typically create value for a visitor seeking information online. However, if you are specific, concise, focus on a particular message, and then provide some context, you will have better luck with your results. You should also be patient and provide feedback to the chatbot to revise the content into what you want—perhaps manually editing the content yourself after it's complete.

With the right prompts, you can use ChatGPT to speed up your productivity with your content and SEO by making requests such as:

- Add visual elements like headings, subheadings, and lists in this article, to break up the content and make it more readable. (Then paste your existing article below the prompt.)

- Modify the length of this article to 400 words.
- Provide me with 3 alternative versions of this article.
- Pretend you are an SEO expert. Develop a strategy to improve the search engine ranking for the following article.
- Provide catchy clickbait blog post titles relating to the list of SEO keywords below.
- Pretend you are a content marketer. Write a catchy meta description for a blog post with keyword 1, keyword 2, and keyword 3 while ensuring that the meta description is 155 characters maximum.

While ChatGPT and other large language models are not a magic bullet to rank better, if you learn how to use it, it can become a very powerful writing assistant to help you write content and optimize that content to reach your goals and convince your target audience to take action.

Image Rich Search

What's exciting (and an opportunity for you) is appearing in more search results using images. In the past, you may have used a reverse image search (uploaded a photo of a dog to determine the dog breed) or performed a simple Google search, and found the included image results were more helpful than text. What can you do to enhance your image ranking, and potentially out-perform your competitors or at least provide a new traffic source to your website?

- **High quality optimized images:** first, the obvious. Use high-quality, well-lit, clear images. While still maintaining quality, properly compress the images to ensure fast loading times.
- **Relevant text:** make sure your image filenames are descriptive as such organic-garden-raised-beds.jpg instead of image001.jpg. Include alt text (alternative text) in your image tags so search engines understand context. Near the image, use captions and descriptions with

appropriate keywords for better web accessibility.

- **Schema markup:** use structured data to help search engines understand your images. For example, you could list images of e-commerce items for sale with the price included, or include a carousel of images representing different cooking steps in a recipe process.

- **Image sitemap:** generate and submit an Image Sitemap to Google to ensure they index all your images that they might not otherwise find, for example, if they are only reached using JavaScript code.

Factor images into your ongoing SEO strategy. Make sure your bases are covered (the fundamentals), monitor changes, and adjust your strategies. Know that Google is working on combining image search with regular search for rich results. Get good at Image SEO.

Voice Search

It's important to optimize your website so that smart speakers such as Google Home and Amazon Echo can provide search results that send people to you.

The key is conversational content and answering questions. When you perform traditional keyword optimization, you may be targeting short phrases such as "best travel destinations in the Caribbean" but a voice search may be something longer and more conversational, such as, "What are some great travel destinations to visit in the Caribbean?" How would searchers phrase a question when speaking?

Create Frequently Asked Questions pages so that you can provide search engines with these short answers, and ideally get listed in the Featured Snippets section. Answers should be concise. There is no "second place" listing in voice search. Also note Google will start pulling answers directly off the page and presenting results versus sharing pages that may have the answer listed on them.

As with other SEO tasks, you should use keyword research tools such as Google Keyword Planner,

SEMrush, and Moz. You can also guide your content creation through voice search tools such as AnswerThePublic and AlsoAsked to target those long-tail conversational phrases. If your business has a local presence, create content about your local landmarks, events, and community topics, or directions to capitalize on these local results.

Research any structured data (schema markup) that can provide helpful results in voice searches. Monitor your results and test voice searches on different smart speaker devices to get an idea of what you rank for, what others rank for, and how your voice search ranking is progressing.

User Stories

We realize that the above may seem like a long, boring, technical list of tasks and requirements for you to apply to your webpages. You are correct! We at EWR Digital can perform a content SEO audit on your site, if you are thinking, "I want to know where my weaknesses are." Or, "I want to fix a few of these issues now."

Here's an idea for you to tackle this problem at a surface level: **user stories.** What would be, not "the" ideal, but "an" ideal start-to-finish journey that a prospect could take to find you?

As an example, let's say you were an enterprise company like Adobe, and someone heard about a "magic eraser" tool available in Photoshop. That curious prospect searches Google for the term "adobe photoshop magic eraser."

The search results include a video, highlighting the exact spot in the video that would be most helpful. The "People Also Ask" section of the search results lists 9 related questions that may lead to the exact answer. Then, the first "blog post" (tutorial) looking entry lists the web page named "Erase parts of an image in Adobe Photoshop." Followed by three sentences that accurately summarize the step-by-step process to use that tool.

If you clicked into that tutorial and onto that web page in Adobe's "help" section, you would be amazed at how quickly the clean and simple web page loaded. You would notice that the web page began with a quick summary and then listed a quick numbered list explaining the steps.

You might notice a live chat icon on the page, a few links and highlighted tips, bolded sub-sections, screenshots and animated GIFs to be as helpful as possible. You could tell just by looking at this random web page that many different writers have thought about this lesson and revised this web page, over perhaps many years to keep it up to date, and looked back over it a number of times to ensure it created a good user experience.

Under the tutorial is a "More like this" section to see other related Photoshop tutorials including different painting tools or brush patterns. Under that, links to buy Adobe Photoshop or signup for a free trial.

Under that, a link to sign in to an existing Adobe account, and under that, a small graphic to register for the latest Adobe conference. Past that, links to legal pages, icons to share the article on social media platforms, a way to provide yes/no feedback if the web page was helpful or not, and additional website navigation beyond that.

Compare that to a "poor" search experience you may have had. What if you were at a trade conference, and you wanted to show off a specific web page of your own to someone you just met?

You don't remember the exact web page you're looking for, so you search on Google. Does the webpage you are looking for appear quickly and easily, with a relevant title and (meta) description?

When you click on that web page, at your crowded conference room with 450 devices connected to hotel wifi or roaming cellular services in an unknown city, how quickly does the page load? You're used to loading the page on your large MacBook Pro screen on your desk, but what about your prospect's Google Pixel phone?

Are you sweating bullets, hoping that this person who's never visited your website before, knows exactly what to do? Is the webpage clean, simple, and intuitive— but also specific? This is where it helps to "battle test" your user's journey and dial-in your on-page SEO efforts.

Keyword Ideas

Another fun exercise to repeat in this user story, perhaps more slowly this time, is from a keyword perspective. You can do this using minimal tools, many of which you probably use on a daily basis— you just don't notice it!

First, do you choose correct keywords? Going back to that example about the "Adobe Photoshop eraser" tool. Autocomplete is present on many smartphone apps and search boxes, that we no longer notice it. Consider this: search Google for "Adobe Photoshop eraser" and then do nothing. Don't click the search button. Stop and see what suggestions appear:

- adobe photoshop eraser tool
- adobe photoshop eraser tool not working
- adobe photoshop eraser tool circle disappeared
- adobe photoshop eraser settings
- adobe photoshop erase background
- adobe photoshop eraser text
- adobe photoshop eraser part of layer
- adobe photoshop magic eraser tool

Do this with a search specific to you and you should get a few ideas from these suggestions, possibly for future similar or more specific articles, or a list like this might give you thoughts about what to add to your existing blog post— or perhaps you already mention some of these specifics, but you should emphasize these sub-topics in your article as you know that these are common search questions.

Next, look at the "People Also Ask" section of the search results— another section you sometimes use without noticing. It lists common questions such as:

- How do I get the magic eraser in Photoshop?
- How does magic eraser work in Photoshop?
- Where is the magic eraser tool in Photoshop CC?
- What is the difference between eraser and magic eraser in Photoshop?
- How do I enable the magic tool in Photoshop?
- Why can't I find the magic eraser?
- How do you activate a magic eraser?
- How do I use the magic eraser tool in? (this is an interesting one, because it tells you that you

might have to show how to find the tool in different versions of the software)

- How do I get my magic eraser to work?
- What is the shortcut key of Magic eraser tool?
- How do I remove part of an image in Photoshop?
- Why is the Magic Eraser not working in Photoshop?

Every one of these questions is your opportunity to answer these questions better than the current "People Also Ask" results. Also, consider this: someone searching might be overwhelmed by the little questions listed, and click into your article to get one of these answers.

You may be looking at these lists, wondering to yourself, "What's the pattern? What are the buckets?" How do you sub-categorize these sorts of keyword ideas to adapt them to your own uses? Consider that your website visitors range from casual browsers, to those looking to "convert"— click on a buy button, email signup button, or whatever a "conversion" might be to you. You can sort your keyword types like this:

- **informational:** someone learns more about a specific topic that relates to your organization
- **navigational:** a visitor looking for a specific site or page of yours or how to get to a specific destination like to your store
- **commercial:** a person researching the "best" solution to their problem if it's a product or service and then comparing solutions, so explain why you're the right fit
- **transactional:** they are ready to "buy" and are looking for a way to do that from you

Hopefully this gives you a starting idea of the art and science we perform for on-page SEO. This is only the beginning, and you can use many tools to check your competitors and "fill the keyword gap."

The goal is to turn simple blog posts into linkable assets. Ask yourself: for every piece of content on your site, why would someone want to link to that? Let's say you had a web page with some detailed research, a tutorial, podcast, case study, or guide that someone could find useful. It's easy to take Google search results for granted— Google is a website that is choosing to link to you. Give them a good reason!

Now that we've covered the bases of making your webpage an appealing "target" for search engines to link to, and a helpful location for your website visitors to land, let's talk about what your webpages will accomplish for you— your call-to-action!

Conversion Rate Optimization (CRO)

When you look at the web pages on your site, how much attention do you pay to the Call to Action (CTA), and the end of your article when you provide your pitch? What do you want someone to do after they have visited and consumed the content on that webpage?

The answer: you want your visitor to convert— in the form of a sale (purchase or transaction), lead generation (opt-in to a newsletter, request a quote, download an e-book), click-through (visit another specific page), submit a form (like a contact form or survey), engage (watch a video, share content, leave a comment), or micro-convert (add to cart, signup for a free trial). For each of your webpages, what is your conversion goal?

Now that we've improved the "low hanging fruit" of the webpage content, technical aspects, and keywords, we can begin the ongoing process of measuring the conversions on your web pages (whatever that means for you) and then apply the following to move the needle and make sure your web pages give you the most results by working on the following...

- **Website analytics:** user behavior, traffic sources, time on page, conversion rates, and heatmaps
- **A/B testing:** split testing webpage "elements" such as headlines, calls-to-action, images
- **Landing page essentials:** strong headline, value proposition, persuasive copy, appealing visuals, a working call-to-action
- **Funnels:** end goal and bottlenecks or barriers where users drop off
- **Trust and social proof:** testimonials, reviews, badges, certifications, logos
- **Clear goals:** phone calls, form fills, downloads, etc.

You may have a few of the above SEO practices in place without realizing, but you can see there's room for improvement in a few ways— many times, for us, it's a matter of just looking at the data and figuring out the micro-steps (checking search rankings, title tags, page load times) and making the small improvements that add up. Because our team eats, sleeps, and breathes data and results driven marketing, we are obsessed with the progress that can be made and many times exceed the goals that are set. You see, not many companies look at their websites constantly and would be surprised by their digital presence and the stuff they are putting out if they took the time. By doing these things you should easily outrank them!

Best Practices

1. **URL structure:** separate the words in your URLs with dashes (-) if possible, instead of underscores or spaces. Make your URLs both concise and descriptive. If it makes sense, arrange your URLs in a logical hierarchy like *example.com/category/page* into subfolders.

2. Monitor your webpages and **update URLs** when necessary, using 301 redirects when changing URLs, to prevent broken links.

3. **Title tags:** keep title tags between 50-60 characters if possible. Avoid spammy wording like excessive ALL CAPS, strange punctuation, or keyword stuffing. Ensure title tags are unique across webpages. Consider vertical bars (|) to separate sections of your title tag.

4. **Page load times:** if possible, ensure your webpages load as close to 2 seconds as possible. You can accomplish this using content delivery networks (CDNs) like WordPress, minimizing redirects, gzip compression, browser caching, minifying CSS, JavaScript, and HTML, and lazy loading graphics.

Chapter 3: Off-Page SEO | Brand Mentions, Guest Blogging, Podcast Guesting, Press Releases

Now that you have cleaned up the minor problems on your existing web pages (perhaps, slow load time or missing legal pages) and you have some awareness of how your pages are performing (through Google Search Console), let's focus on the links coming back to your site— off-page search engine optimization!

We like to think about off-page SEO as networking or votes. Who is already linking to you? Who should be linking to you? Who is linking to your competitors?

If you've tried SEO before and failed, or were unhappy with the results, you could have been missing a team that was constantly thinking about your situation, and putting in the daily work (time) to get you to your goals.

If your SEO team is in-house and only works on SEO one hour per week, or only thinks about it once every two months, you are behind. Imagine you had two, five, ten, or more people working on getting you backlinks and social shares, winning the "popularity" contest of your site. What recurring tasks would they be doing for you?

Off-page SEO is about building the authority, reputation, and relevance outside your website. Your goals are visibility, increased organic traffic, and better search engine rankings.

Many times, with link building, people ask us, "Can I buy or spam links?" which is very 5 and 10 years ago thinking, and just a bad practice. Search engine guidelines very much recommend against buying links, and even if this was a strategy you were to try, it's more expensive and time-consuming to be worth the effort. If a website is popular, well-respected, and has many incoming links— like a link from a government (.gov) website, or is perhaps a huge news organization like Time Magazine— search engines see that as a more valuable link to you that you "earned", compared to a "bad neighborhood" site linking to you with random links all over the place and probably to many other low quality sites with tons of low quality links as well. Next, logical thinking asks, "Should I link to my site from various social media profiles?" This is a step in the right direction, but it's playing it safe— thinking too small. While you should have social media profiles on Facebook, LinkedIn, Twitter, Instagram, Pinterest, and so on, it's not going to help your off-page SEO as much as you think.

Many social sites including Facebook and Twitter hesitate to promote off-page links in their searches or feeds. You should also note that social media sites want engaging posts— content that gets people to like, comment, and watch. Their goal is to keep their users on their site, not get them to click off to your site. Also, it's good to note that Google is trying to measure sentiment and relevance and looks at where your post reforms and what types of people are engaging with it as well as what they are saying.

Also, consider those times you found a company's Facebook page, and there was zero engagement... just post after post, linking to different blog posts. Your social presence is something to focus on— definitely have accounts and post regularly— but these signals are a small part of off-page SEO.

What moves the needle when it comes to off-page SEO? Networking and Authority building! As in, building relationships and following up with people who can link to you, instead of looking for short-sighted tricks or static posting. This is why you need a team (like ours) that can perform community engagement and constant outreach and follow-up. Here's what could be done...

Brand Mentions

Is it possible there are websites out there that talk about you, but don't link to you? Let's say you were ZenDesk, a software-as-a-service company that hosts help-desk software.

ZenDesk might be mentioned in blog posts talking about helpful business resources, ranking help desk software specifically, or shown in countless YouTube tutorials. These are all untapped resources! Imagine if a team regularly checked the internet for websites mentioning ZenDesk, found the appropriate contact information, and asked the webmasters of these sites to update the blog post with a link back to ZenDesk.

You may have tried searching your own company or brand to see who mentions you, but does not link back. You may have a Google Alert or Mention for your company name to see what new results appear. However, imagine if a team combed through thousands of search results for your company name, sorted (tagged) them to remove the irrelevant results, and constantly worked through this "outreach" list of brand mentions.

You aren't limited to your home page or one specific page of your site, either. Perhaps you find that blog post mentioning your organization, and you have a specific web page that could use a link.

Here's an example: you find a blog post explaining the top 10 help desk solutions, and your SaaS company, ZenDesk, is only ranked at number four. They incorrectly state that your software is missing an important feature or has some other limitation. You could contact that webmaster and ask them to update their article and link to your blog post that explains that feature of your help desk software.

You could monitor the keywords of your competitors. If you find a site that reviews help desk solutions or provides a list of the "best ones"— and yours is not listed— ask if the website will update their post and mention your company. Better yet, if you know a company on that list that has gone out of business you can highlight that and get your business added to those round-up posts. This is one of the most effective strategies we have used with some of our bigger clients that don't have thousands of dollars to spend on Public Relations.

Check Broken Links

When the average person talks about checking for broken links, they limit their thinking to on-page SEO, asking, "Do the internal and external links on my site go where they're supposed to?"

With off-page SEO, you can use special tools to check the broken links of other sites. What if a website reviewed a solution of some kind that has changed their website link or a news article that has taken down that article and it's now producing a 404 not found error?

Contact the webmaster about the broken link and ask if it can be changed to the appropriate updated link to maybe your site with a similar offering. That blog post could be an important piece of content for that site, providing backlinks and search rankings to them. They don't want to delete the entire post, leave the outgoing link broken, or do a lot work rewriting that blog post. You are making it easy for them!

However, how easy is it for you? Back to small thinking, if you only had one person on this case, only thinking or working on this intermittently, you wouldn't make a lot of progress. But if you had our team at your disposal, working on a list of websites every day, marking those web pages that weren't interested in changing the link, or were unresponsive and required follow-up later, do you see how you could notice measurable progress every month, with a series of small "wins"— more and more webpages linking directly to you? Note also that one high quality link could be worth 100 lower quality links or more. Now that is working smarter, not harder!

Reputation Management

Speaking of monitoring, let's go back to basics and think about which websites (organizations) Google wants to reward, and those it would punish. If you didn't care about your site— how fast it loaded, how accurate and up-to-date it was, what people said about you— why would Google want to rank you highly in their search results?

You may have also thought about how "deep" or "shallow" some of these relationships need to be. For example, do you set a quota of contacting 25 brand mentions per day, or 50 broken links per day? Is it just a numbers game?

In addition to the above superficial tasks, you'll want to perform deep research. Perhaps when you were checking brand mentions, you noticed websites say good and bad things about you. Depending on what your organization does, it would be a good idea to regularly check product review sites, Amazon, Yelp, TripAdvisor, NextDoor. Consider sites like Capterra, G2, TrustPilot, and GlassDoor. It's easy for you to get "stuck" in the same handful of websites and social media websites you visit, forgetting that so many review sites exist and people do use them! Not to mention, if your organization has an app, what about the Apple App Store, Google Play Store, Samsung Galaxy Store, and Microsoft Store?

When you search "EWR Digital" you can see that we are listed on many review sites including the Better Business Bureau, Clutch, Upcity, and many others.

The obvious benefit for you checking review sites is to clean up bad reviews, or be aware of what people are saying about you, but it's still worth it to check out the relevant review sites for a few other reasons.

How would you feel about a company listed on a review site or an app store, yet had no ratings or reviews? This is your chance to claim your business listing (more about this when we discuss Google My Business in the local SEO chapter), see how your competitors are rated, and use that as motivation to funnel your customers to these review sites. Software tools exist where you can ask your recent customers to survey their experience with your company. If they leave a bad experience, you can redirect them to your customer service team to fix the problem. But if they leave a favorable review, you can send them to these review sites to re-enter their favorable review. While they are good, you also want to look at Google policies to make sure this review software follows all guidelines, or you could get into trouble.

Guest Blogging

The most impactful recurring task you could have your off-site SEO team perform is guest blogging, which means you publish content on high-reputation websites in your industry. Just make sure that site does not require money for you to post content with them, as that is against the Google guidelines and they pretty much know what sites do that— those links will have no value beyond the referral traffic you may get from it.

When you Google search your name, or a high-profile person in your organization, what results appear, besides your own sites and social media profiles? When you Google my name, Matt Bertram, the first few pages include results on Search Engine Journal, Entrepreneur Magazine, Forbes, and our top rated SEO podcast.

Is your mind already overwhelmed with the series of interconnected steps required to make this happen? Wonderful— that's why most people don't take action and follow-through, and why you can, when you have a team like ours do the work for you. Just imagine the do-able steps required to make this happen:

- Our team looks at your industry, your competitors, and your organization to determine which publications to contact.
- We look at each of those high-profile websites to understand their typical content, and also find a gap your content can fill (for example, Search Engine Journal has an "Enterprise SEO" category, so I published a guest blog post there about Enterprise SEO for SaaS brands.
- We contact these websites to begin a relationship, ask if they currently accept guest blog posts, and obtain their editorial guidelines.
- We follow-up if the webmaster doesn't reply, or if they have replied, with a list of quick ideas (pitches) for guest blog post topics.

- We follow-up again with that fully written guest blog post, our bio, and photos.
- When the article goes live, we promote the guest blog post on every channel we control (social media channels, a post about it on our own site, email blast, and maybe a press release) to co-promote ourselves and the guest blog website.

Since the internet began, it has been all about sharing and mutual beneficial relationships. Why did people post on forums or leave blog comments? Why do you post articles on your LinkedIn page, and why does LinkedIn promote your content? Why do you live stream into your Facebook group, and so on? The answer is that you contribute in a small way to a large website, and in return, you are rewarded with a small amount of their traffic and new connections.

Any high-reputation website is always in need of new content, and if you can deliver what their readers want— and promote your guest content through your own channels— you win in a way that most people just don't understand. You should be building these prospect lists of referral sources, marketing (your guest blog post pitch), refining that pitch so it delivers the value that site wants, following up, delivering, and then continuously promoting that content once it's published.

Just think about all the ways you benefit from guest posting. Your credibility is improved by being featured in these publications. The publication sends traffic to you and your site just by virtue of having so much traffic of their own. These are already high-ranking websites, so your name and search keywords help you dominate the first page of Google. When you promote this guest content on your own platforms, you also impress your viewers— you aren't promoting your own websites, you're promoting your content that was so good, these high-reputation websites listed it.

This does not happen magically— it does require planning, a lot of labor, being organized (replying and following up), and an ongoing strategy (promoting your guest article forever) but this is what serious enterprise businesses do when they want to build their digital presence.

Podcast Guesting

When we talk about internet reciprocity, sharing, and collaboration, you might think about podcasting, and specifically, podcast guesting. To get us both on the same page, a podcast is an online radio show, consisting of long-form audio episodes, published on a regular basis (usually weekly or twice-monthly), and usually ten minutes to three hours in length.

A solo-cast, or a podcast that publishes one person monologuing, or even a host and co-host setup, is great, but can easily become repetitive, running out of ideas. The format of some shows are entirely "host and guest" every episode, or some in-house podcasts occasionally accept guests to keep the content fresh.

For example, I help run OGGN (Oil and Gas Global Network)— a podcast network, meaning a collection of podcasts under one umbrella all focused on the oil and gas industry. We have shows like Oil & Gas This Week, hosted by Paige Wilson and Mark LaCour, a weekly news show that mostly features the same two guests every week and is consistently rated the top oil and gas podcast in the world.

We also have interview shows like Oil and Gas Digital Doers, and Oil and Gas Industry Leaders— where we interview C-level executives. This format works great for everyone involved. We always get new content from our guests, in areas of the industry we might not cover. It's a networking opportunity for both us and our guests. Audiences also love it, because it never gets stale. Consider how many television talk shows, or radio interview shows, have existed for decades, almost effortlessly. Their secret? A steady supply of guests! *(Shameless Plug Alert: If you are an inhouse marketer or salesperson or sales manager you should check my podcast even if you are not in oil and gas with the founder Mark LaCour called, "Oil and Gas Sales and Marketing Podcast" which delivers a lot of useful content as it relates to how sales and marketing should work together more closely and is currently ranked as one of the top 15 best oil and gas podcasts!)*

Podcasts benefit your off-page SEO because your episode is distributed to many podcast platforms like Apple Podcasts, Google Podcasts, Spotify, iHeartRadio, and more— in addition to the main podcast website where your episode is hosted. If the podcast where you guest records you on video, the show will probably post on YouTube and as video posts on their social media channels, which you should re-post and share.

Many podcasts also repurpose your content as tweets, quote graphics (for Pinterest and Instagram), audiograms (audio clips mixed with a still image for video), reels (video clips for Instagram, TikTok, YouTube Shorts, Facebook Reels), and sometimes reformat parts of the transcribed interview into blog posts for Medium and LinkedIn. Podcast guesting combines the benefits of content marketing and guest blog posting, although podcast guesting is perhaps more quantity than quality than guest blogging. I believe it's one of the best ways today to share your story, let people get to know you better and hopefully buy from you as well create high quality content that can be repurposed. If you are not guest podcasting or podcasting yourself, you should consider starting!

Imagine how a team like our team could market you on podcasts:

- We build that initial list of high-profile podcasts based on your industry and your competitors who also appear on podcasts.

- We pitch these podcasts using a slightly customized template to pass along your bio (speaker one-sheet), possible podcast guest appearances, and help the podcast host understand the value you bring to their show.

- We follow-up with non-responsive prospects until they give us a "yes" or "no"— at which point you are scheduled for your podcast interview— you usually choose a time and date on their online scheduler and appear for a Zoom meeting.

- We follow-up after the show to gather feedback, confirm publication dates, and continue the conversation.

- When your episode is live, we promote the episode consistently on your social channels, forever, as part of your content library. If there are repurposed artifacts as mentioned above— graphics, video clips, audio, text— we can post those as well.

Influencer Marketing, Press Releases & More

We can repeat this thought process in other avenues. What prospects should you reach, to get back to your website? Who can help us raise your profile? Based on these connectors (referral sources), what value can you add with your content? Contact, follow-up, get to a successful goal, follow-up again, market, and repeat.

If it's appropriate for your niche and your goals, we can build your off-page SEO with **influencer marketing:** contact social media personalities, bloggers, industry experts who can promote your organization through sponsored content, product reviews, or affiliate marketing.

We also love using **press releases** to promote our company, EWR Digital. We used them when we rebranded our company name, when we were recognized at the Better Business Bureau, Crystal and the Manifest, and Hermes Creative awards, and when we landed OGGN as a strategic partner.

When your organization has something noteworthy (newsworthy) about your recent activities that you believe deserves media coverage (you can look at the press releases your competitors release to get ideas), you structure this announcement with a catchy headline, informative body copy, and contact information. Then reach out to media contacts and slightly personalize the press release for each outlet. It's even easier when you use a press release distribution service to send this out.

Now that you have a start with on-page and off-page SEO, let's turn our attention to the next logical step in the process, which combines both techniques: local SEO— where you claim local business listings, rank for local keywords, create local content, build up online reviews, and build local links.

Chapter 4: Local Search Engine Optimization

Search engine optimization is all about getting you more visibility, and you need to keep local SEO in mind as a factor for two simple reasons: search engines reward you for being a local result, and your competitors are operating with the "local" mindset, whether you are, or not.

I remember back in the day if a lawyer in New York or California had good SEO they would dominate the search results, which is okay I guess, but what if you were a plumber and there were results coming up for a plumbing company that does not even service your area? You can see how this would not be ideal and would frustrate users.

Local Search Algorithm 3-Pack

With local SEO, consider these three factors: Proximity, Prominence, and Relevance.

Proximity: Google knows the zip code of their visitors, and possibly even exact GPS coordinates if searching from a mobile device. When they search, and possibly see your business in the results, you would expect Google (and similar search engines) to prefer nearby locations.

Prominence: Your local reputation is important in local search results. If someone searches "hairdresser The Woodlands Texas" then Google will look at the online visibility and reputation compared to other local businesses. Also, how many searches and different formats of your name are people searching, compared to others in that category?

They calculate overall online authority by looking at quantity, consistency, and quality of reviews, online citations (mention of that business name, address, and phone number on other websites), activity on the Google My Business / Google Business Profile page (viewers reading reviews and other details of things like your mini blog posts and FAQ's), and local foot traffic or driving direction requests. Google tracks everything, including when users check-in or when their GPS coordinates overlap yours.

Relevance: Google might compare the specific keywords a local user searches with your business name, category, on-page SEO, and keywords used in reviews. In other words, ensure your keywords match the keywords you want local users to search.

Listings, Off-Page, On-Page

The low-hanging fruit with your local SEO strategy centers around Google My Business— the free tool that allows you to manage your Search and Maps listings, including elements such as your address, phone number, business category, and photos.

To understand SEO at a local level, try searching for terms like "chiropractor" or "handyman" to find local businesses with their local search listing dialed-in. Then, when you notice one of those businesses with many reviews, try Googling that business name directly (with your browser location enabled) followed by your city's name, to see what features appear in Google's local listing sidebar. You will observe the following...

Local Search Results

The local business shows a map of their service area, their hours, phone, website, reviews, links to social media profiles.

Claim your listing on Google Business Profile, then claim your business anywhere else you can— Yelp, and Bing Places, for example. Fully complete these local profiles. Consider two competing local businesses, with nearly identical offers, reviews, and web pages. One fills out only a few areas of their profile, while the other completes all fields. Who has the advantage?

You should regularly monitor your claimed local listings. It is common sense that you should check reviews and respond to them, but very few companies think to check their business listing after setting it up.

If your phone number, office hours, and address in Google don't match your website, it appears untrustworthy. If you posted the most recent photo on your business listing 4 years ago, that looks out-of-date. Post videos. Add a FAQ and mini-blogs. Fill in every section you can as often as you can.

Add many images to your local directory listing. The "average" business owner only thinks to post a quick image of the outside, the inside, and perhaps a menu. However, think about a time you (or a friend) researched a local business using an app like Yelp. Three images are not enough for someone to make an informed decision or to recognize that location once they've arrived. Consider any advantage your competitor might have over you— perhaps they've posted 15 or 30 images around their establishment. Post lots of pictures of your team, brand, and with customers, and from different angles of the outside of the business and make sure you post them across the local directory platforms.

Do you wonder how some businesses get hundreds or thousands of reviews? The secret is that they funnel their customers and clients through that review process. Are you following up with your buyers to get reviews on your local listings?

Local Link Building

It does not end with Google and Bing local listings. That local website might have claimed listings on Yelp, Yellow Pages, Nextdoor, MapQuest, Chamber of Commerce, Moovit, ZoomInfo, Yahoo! Search — whatever is relevant to their industry. If you click into any of these review sites, you'll see a full profile filled out for that business listing (about section, website and email links, recent reviews, many reviews, and photos).

Include these additional review sites as part of your recurring plan to claim local listings, regularly check your profiles to ensure they match, updating with content (mini-blogs, videos, audios). Encourage and respond to reviews on these sites.

Add lots of images. Think back to times when you have used local review sites such as Yelp or Nextdoor to research a local restaurant or contractor. Which profiles look like they were setup one-time, many years ago? Which look like they are maintained on a monthly basis by a team?

Some companies will try to charge you a monthly fee to maintain your NAP and citations— this could be a waste of money if you are not trying to get these directories to change your location. They may be worth it in the instance that you may have recently changed locations and you don't have the login anymore. Just make sure your SEO team is aware of where your business is listed, what is listed, and how often they maintain those results. This is where audits are helpful.

Google wants you to be hyper-active in your community. Links from sites in the industry (in which you are an expert) help, but if your focus is on local search engine results, do anything you can to get listed in local directories (Yelp and the rest listed above), Chamber of Commerce, and local news sites.

Local On-Page SEO

When you search for a local business in your area, and you click into the website itself, and you'll see that it mentions locally relevant information such as specific cities serviced— there are most likely pages dedicated to specific cities, showing information specific to that location.

What is a popular gas station near you, perhaps Shell? If you searched "shell gas stations near me" or "shell gas station" followed by your city name— the Google results show photos of that location, the price of gas there, and so on. You could click into a web page dedicated specifically to that location, listing the exact address, features (i.e. ATM, EV charging), GPS coordinates and operating hours. Even a gas station creates pages for every location. If your business has multiple locations, create a page for each location so you can optimize for each one.

When you edit your page, make sure your target keywords are relevant to your Google Business Profile (GBP) page as well as having unique and helpful content.

You need a high-quality, fast-loading web page that is linked to your GBP. Think about your "Core Web Vitals" and what your team can do to get these pages loading in just a few seconds.

If your CMS (Content Management System, such as WordPress) allows it, investigate the structured data you can add to these local web pages. Structured data contains additional details (metadata) about your pages such as the website's author, physical address, GPS coordinates, phone number, operating hours, and more. These are invisible to people visiting your web page, but are indexed by the search engines. This way, users can see details about your business (and these specific local pages) directly on Google, before they click to your site.

This also gives you benefits with voice search— if your structured data clearly defines your hours of operation, for example, then someone can ask on their smart speaker (Google Home, Alexa, Siri, or Google Assistant) what time your business opens.

You can enjoy a boost in your search engine visibility when you take local SEO seriously as studies say that maps currently represent about one-third of the current search traffic— and chances are you'll find a few factors that are currently limiting your local search results, allowing your competition to get ahead. Be aware of the actions you need to make the most of your local search engine optimization listings.

Search engine optimization does not have to be that complicated — it simply has a lot of moving parts, and requires your team's recurring attention. You may begin to understand how some SEO agencies give you superficial wins only (i.e. monitoring keyword rankings or claiming your Google My Business local listings), which are important, but you also need a consistent strategy to make these efforts worthwhile.

Do not skip over the fundamentals. The ideas behind SEO build on the previous: on-page, off-page, and local. EWR Digital excels at tying together your goals of marketing, web development, user experience, and branding. This may involve multiple websites, legacy systems, many different people and departments — and possibly multiple store locations — so let's talk about how you can scale your business, your website, and your traffic with SEO.

Local SEO Checklist

1. **Claim and verify your Google My Business listing, along with other local search engines like Bing Places.** Fill in any detail you can and be sure your business name, address, phone number, website URL, business hours, and categories are accurate, up-to-date, and uniform across all platforms. Direct your customers to these pages to increase your reviews. Regularly update these listings with posts and photos.

2. **Get listed in local directories.** Where applicable, get every location in your business listed in directories like Yelp, Yellow Pages, and anywhere else the organizations in your industry should be listed. Make sure these listings provide the same information and that you update them regularly.

3. **Local keyword research.** Identify relevant local search terms and incorporate them into your website content, meta tags, and headings.

4. **Reviews and reputation.** Respond to both positive and negative reviews about your company when your customers post them.

Search by Matthew Bertram

Chapter 5: Enterprise Search Engine Optimization

How do you apply the SEO principles we've talked about so far, and promote your site at a large scale?

As an enterprise-level organization, what challenges do you face that you would not otherwise experience with the SEO on a smaller site? Which of these enterprise SEO issues are a struggle for your enterprise organization?

- **legacy issues:** poor technical foundations such as unclean data caused by years of code additions, URL restructuring, employee turnover over many years.
- **content quality:** neglected, poor quality, and duplicate content sometimes caused by auto-generated non-unique content.
- **crawlability and indexability:** search engines miss the new, valuable content you want indexed because they are excessively crawling too many low-quality or auto-generated URLs.

- **corporate environments:** navigate internal politics to champion SEO goals, persuade decision-makers and tell compelling stories based on the data— work with different departments and geographic areas to get buy-in from multiple teams.

- **website scale:** understand and manage one huge website or several smaller websites that work together.

- **identify issues:** maintain an efficient, top-level view of performance and technical health to detect issues before they arise and mitigate errors— an increase in non-indexable pages, server errors, broken links, high fetch times, improper use of hreflang and other tags and duplicate content— identify these by scheduling regular crawls.

Thinking about these several problems, it can be difficult for you to know where to begin. The way forward is to develop a plan, then seek quick wins so you can get buy-in from your company's teams, make SEO a part of your culture, and make sure everyone is involved.

This is an ongoing process that requires a strategic approach to overcome the unique challenges your organization faces— mostly, the problem of "scale"— there is so much to figure out and many people to involve. Here are the factors we suggest you examine:

- **access:** figure out internal access, legacy systems, and company culture.
- **workflow and approvals:** everyone in your organization should understand SEO within their context, working together to speak better with the search engines.
- **scale and complexity:** ensure your many pages are properly indexed, optimized, and maintained.
- **site architecture:** revise your website so that it's well-structured with clear navigation. This means a logical hierarchy and effective internal linking.
- **keyword research:** instead of leaving keyword ranking and results to chance, you target relevant search terms that match your business goals and attract high-intent traffic.
- **content strategy:** use diverse content formats like blog posts, videos, and infographics to

engage users and give them the answers to the problems they were searching for— align with their "search intent."

- **technical SEO:** address technical issues including speed, performance, mobile friendliness, crawlability (telling search engines to stay away from low-quality pages that should not be crawled), and sitemaps.
- **multi-location SEO:** apply local SEO strategies to each of your company's locations so you remain visible in search results.
- **competitor analysis:** analyze your competitors' ongoing SEO efforts, growth, and results to identify new opportunities and stay ahead of the competition.
- **monitoring and analytics:** regularly check SEO metrics and performance indicators to create educated data-driven decisions, instead of guesses.

When you look at the big picture in this way, you can apply everything we've explained about SEO into your plan. There may be several problems to identify and solve, but once you solve those problems at scale, you can enjoy massive results at scale.

International SEO

If your organization is based in multiple countries, there are a few additional factors to consider:

- **language:** translate content into different languages if your organization has reach in multiple countries. When translating, also consider cultural and linguistic differences that apply to different regions.

- **country-specific targeting:** register ccTLD's (country code top-level domains) such as example.fr for France, example.ca for Canada, and so on, for content specific to that country. You can also setup your geotargeting in the Google Search Console. Hosting your website on servers located in the target country can also improve local search rankings.

- **geotargeting and hreflang tags:** use special HTML tags (hreflang) to specify the language and regional targeting. This ensures search engines display the correct version of your content to the appropriate audience.

- **local keyword research:** understand how your target audience searches for your products or services in different regions and adapt your keywords accordingly.

- **local business listings:** claim and optimize your profiles on local business directories and search engines to improve your local visibility in each country, state, or city.
- **outreach:** build relationships with local influencers and websites to acquire high-quality backlinks from region-specific sources.
- **user experience:** tailor your website experience to each target audience that applies, including language, currency, and localized content.
- **country manager:** as you move into different areas, hire local experts to help you navigate everything you need to know about this new area.

These "to-do lists" should make you aware of what you have already accomplished (but perhaps should revisit), unsolved problems you know about, and unknown issues you need to solve soon. Search engine optimization (whether enterprise-level, international, local, off-page, or on-page) is all about covering your bases. Without deep thinking and a detailed plan, your efforts devolve into chaos and you neglect important categories.

SEO Tools

SEO teams use multiple tools to stay on top of the work that needs to be done, even if there is overlap in the data these tools provide. Here are just some of the tools we prefer when dealing with optimization and conversion...

- **Google Search Console (free):** check indexing status, keyword rankings, technical issues, quality status, and Core Web Vitals. You can check the status of your entire website or inspect the status of a single webpage.
- **Google Analytics:** analyze traffic, audience demographics, user behavior (pages visited, visit duration, actions taken), conversion rates, and generate custom reporting.
- **Google Keyword Planner (within Google Ads):** research keywords and create keyword strategies for your campaigns. Check search volume, competition level, keyword variations, bid estimates, and historical data.

- **SEMrush:** run a site audit to detect potential issues, track ranking, and analyze competitors, in addition to keyword research and reporting.

- **Ahrefs:** analyze backlinks (number of backlinks, referring domains, and the authority of linking websites), search for trending topics (Content Explorer), check your SEO metrics and top-performing pages (Site Explorer), identify where your competitors rank (Content Gap Analysis), and set alerts— based on gained or lost backlinks, changes in keyword ranking, and changes to competitor websites.

- **Moz Pro:** research keywords, audit your site, track rankings, analyze links, and get recommendations about possible on-page SEO improvements.

- **Moz Local:** manage your site's local listings across many online directories (including Google My Business), monitor reviews, and see how you perform in local search results.

- **Yoast SEO (WordPress):** analyze your content for keyword targeting and readability. Customize how your site appears in search engines (meta titles, descriptions, and schema markup). Suggest internal links. Set canonical

URLs to avoid duplicate content issues. Generate XML sitemaps to ensure all your content is properly indexed.

Although I don't expect you to be an expert in all these search engine optimization (SEO) tools, I hope this gives you a better understanding about what tools would be a good starting point for you to start improving your SEO presence.

SEO Hosting

Google doesn't care who your web host is, but they care about speed, uptime, reliability, and security. When you are at the enterprise level, your hosting situation may be complex and unique, with configurations such as...

- multiple websites with different domain names and IP addresses, linking together.
- unique and regional IP addresses located in various neighborhoods (i.e. the US, Africa, France).

- server uptime and performance (fast page loads), including alerts to notify your team about any downtime issues.
- **clean IP addresses:** keep your website addresses off of blacklists, especially when email deliverability is important.
- **crawl rate optimization:** control the rate at which search engine bots crawl your large website.
- **Content Delivery Network (CDN):** distribute content (especially static files) across various servers to ensure fast loading times— platforms such as Cloudflare, Akamai, or Amazon CloudFront as well as improved security.

Traditional hosting is focused on server resources (disk space, memory, bandwidth) but SEO-focused hosting infrastructure takes your search engine ranking needs into account. We use Cohosta.com.

The goal is to rank you for relevant keywords and search queries that attract qualified traffic to your site— readers converting into customers. Enterprise SEO is more complex than traditional SEO, and requires strategies that work together, and this is why it's so important that you find a trustworthy enterprise SEO service provider such as EWR Digital that is used to dealing with these bigger projects and potential issues.

Conclusion: EWR Digital & Our Layering Methodology | Align, Elevate, Amplify, Convert

What are your unique enterprise SEO needs and challenges? EWR Digital has a deep understanding of what needs to be done to overcome your fears and frustrations.

If you have tried and failed in the past, you feel like your SEO goals are falling short, not making progress, or you lack clear goals, perhaps your issue is not fully an "action" problem— but more so, a "thinking" problem!

You understand that many aspects of your business require recurring thinking: carefully examining your current setup (your website, search rankings, page load times, content library), then researching and developing strategies about what to change, add, remove, and prioritize. Many times, our team will make website changes and not see the results until weeks or months later.

Some goals require long-term work— re-visiting ideas multiple times. We may work to increase search engine rankings, traffic, conversions, website load times, or compliance issues. We may be searching keywords, content ideas, updating content, or working on various forms of outreach and link building. Some of these goals require multiple attempts over time (fixing that website issue) or require consistent maintenance (outranking others in search engine results).

Just think about how difficult all the moving parts of enterprise SEO would be if you only re-visited your progress, goals, actions, and results "every once in a while"— you would get "once in a while" results.

Something else to consider is that we are SEO specialists. We stay well-informed about industry best practices, do's-and-don'ts, common mistakes, and cutting-edge opportunities. When you have us on your team, you no longer have to switch gears (and mindsets) between your current business and focus, back and forth with your SEO and website goals.

That sounds like a wonderful plan, but how do we make that happen for you? Using our EWR methodology: Strategy, Align, Elevate, Amplify, and Convert.

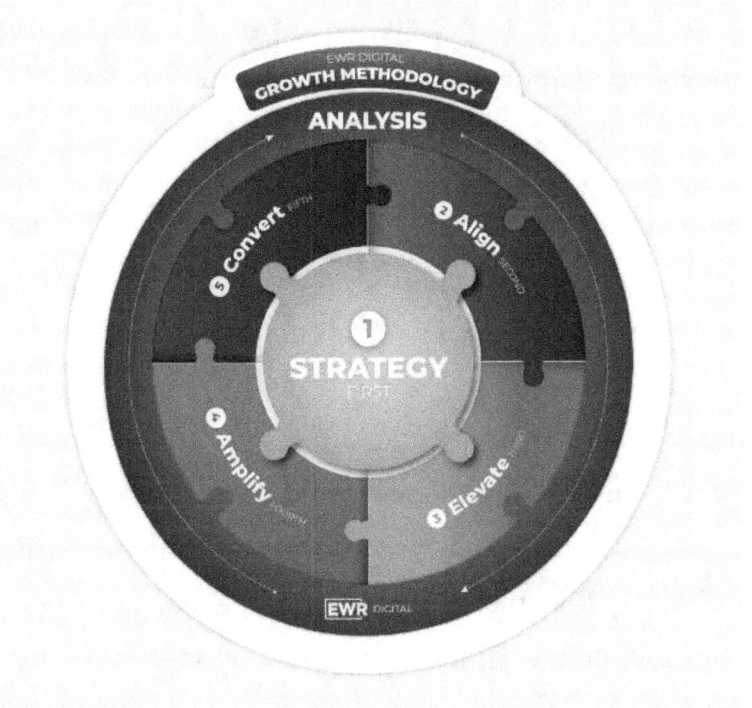

We optimize your website to enhance user experience, implement digital marketing campaigns, leverage your social media platforms— to maximize your online visibility, expand your reach, and drive meaningful conversions.

Our marketing methodology is a structured approach to planning and executing our marketing activities and campaigns.

We begin by defining our business goals and identifying our target audience, which allows us to create messaging and content that resonates with your customers.

From there, we develop a multi-channel marketing strategy that incorporates tactics such as content marketing, social media, email marketing, and search engine optimization, among others. We continually monitor and measure the success of our marketing efforts, using data and feedback to refine our strategies and optimize our performance. By following this methodology, we are able to create effective, efficient marketing campaigns that help us reach your target audience, generate leads, and drive revenue growth.

Strategy

Are your SEO efforts sometimes disjointed, unclear, or ineffective? To overcome this, we have a strong emphasis on strategy. We want to make sure your marketing campaigns are well-planned, well-researched, and well-executed to achieve your results. This includes...

- **marketing plan development:** we created a detailed roadmap for you, detailing the marketing strategies and tactics to put in place, in what order of importance, and on what timeline.

- **market research:** we research your market landscape, target audience, and competition, so the plan is based on reality and what exists.

- **competitor analysis:** we analyze your competitors' strengths, weaknesses, and marketing strategies.

- **brand positioning:** we ensure the strategy sets you apart from your competitors and makes you stand out in the marketplace.

Align

Making plans and making progress is a wonderful start, but we want to make sure these changes fit into the rest of your business and marketing efforts. Our goal is to give you a cohesive brand image and message across all channels. This way, you present a consistent, clear, and aligned brand message to your prospective leads. We accomplish this using these components...

- **brand guidelines:** we make sure your marketing communications are consistent with your brand identity and positioning.
- **marketing and audit workshops:** based on your current marketing efforts, we identify areas for improvement and re-examine how that matches with your business objectives.
- **customer persona development:** we create detailed profiles of your target audience so we can be sure your market efforts communicate with the right people.
- **customer journey:** now that we are aware of your own messaging and ideal customer, we

map out that customer's process— from initial awareness, to becoming a loyal customer.

Elevate

We are committed to taking your company beyond the ordinary through increased visibility, engagement, and conversions. Content is a huge part of search engine optimization, but it means nothing unless we optimize and improve those marketing efforts. We develop high quality content to promote your business, optimize your websites for a better user experience, and use email marketing to keep your visitors engaged. This involves...

- **website design and development:** we make sure your website showcases your products and services, provides helpful information to your visitors, and engages them with an ideal user experience.
- **SEO (search engine optimization):** we perform steps to improve your web pages ranking and visibility on search engines.
- **content marketing:** we develop high-quality, valuable content that educates, entertains, and

engages your target audience— positioning you as the industry thought leader.

- **email marketing:** we develop email campaigns to nurture (follow-up) your leads so that they remain active recurring visitors and remain up-to-date about your activities.

Convert

Your company's SEO efforts make sure the website performs correctly, ranks well, and brings in traffic, in service of the goal: conversion. Specifically, conversion rate optimization, sales funnel optimization, and lead generation. We want to you to see results and growth (return on investment). We focus on the following areas...

- **CRO (conversion rate optimization):** we identify and analyze the bottlenecks on your site where users can convert better— to generate more leads and sales for you.
- **retargeting or remarketing:** we run ads targeting people who have previously interacted with your website or brand.

- **A/B testing:** we compare two versions of your most important web pages to measure the better engaging or better converting variation.
- **heat mapping:** we use a color-coded map to display user behavior on your website, to get insights into where they click and engage with your content.

Search engines use over 200+ ranking factors just to decide how to rank your site. Their algorithm constantly changes (The Google Dance), and we are always learning and implementing ways to ensure you continue to win— despite the many changes. There is always a list of tasks we can perform on your site, off your site, on other platforms, and using outside the box publicity strategies to ensure your organization is the best it can be, and presents itself as best it can.

If it all seems overwhelming, just focus on whatever level of granularity that makes you comfortable. You don't necessarily need to know about schema markup and meta tags, just that we can make changes to your site's output to better help search engines understand you. You don't need to be fully aware of Core Web

Vitals, just that Google rewards you with a faster website.

You can also appreciate the need to monitor review sites talking about you, keep your social media updated with relevant news and photos, and the need for publicity in the form of guest blog posts or press releases, to keep authoritative sites linking to you in regards to your organization's recent news. That leads to the question, how do we work with you to make this happen?

Three Paths: Advisory, Consultative, Collaborative

We are dedicated to helping you achieve your business goals in one of three possible paths:

Advisory. Get a second opinion on your marketing strategy. We would discuss your needs and goals, and you could ask questions about our services. Most importantly, you would know the next steps to take after we have identified potential issues and opportunities. We have one-on-one consulting pages for this offered on our website that you can buy.

Consultative. We could audit your company's marketing objectives, marketing mix (product, price, place, promotion), target markets, marketing research, marketing organization, and marketing budget. We might review external factors such as competition, industry trends, and legal/regulatory issues that may affect the company's marketing efforts.

An SEO audit will help you answer these questions:

- Does my website have technical issues that need to be addressed?
- What factors are contributing to the drop in my rankings?
- Is my content well written and structured correctly?
- Which sites are referring links to my website?
- Do I provide a great user experience on my website?

Auditing should not be a one-time event. You should regularly monitor your website's analytics and keyword rankings to stay competitive. We can help you identify low traffic, traffic loss, slow pages, outdated content, low conversions, and ranking lower than your competitors. We'll look at your on-page, off-page, technical SEO, local SEO, and enterprise issues to create a recommended actions plan based on the known best practices in the SEO industry.

Collaborative. Finally, we could become an active partner to optimize your website and digital marketing efforts. We would collaborate with you to define a shared vision, understand your brand identity and goals.

We would work with you to execute campaigns, content, and improvements— remaining in constant communication to discuss progress, insights, and strategy adjustments— to ensure your campaign remains aligned with your evolving needs.

Contact us today for a free consultation. You can develop great products and services for your enterprise organization, but without website traffic that converts, you're fighting an uphill battle to generate revenue.

Our professionals have a solid grasp of marketing and SEO. We would love to take the time to learn more about your business and determine if we are the correct fit for each other:

MatthewBertram.com

EWRDigital.com

LinkedIn.com/in/mattbertramlive

Unknown Secrets of Internet Marketing Podcast

About Matthew Bertram

Matthew Bertram is a trusted voice in digital strategy—a seasoned marketer, keynote speaker, and host of multiple top-ranked sales and marketing podcasts that have charted in the **Top 15 across multiple categories**.

With over two decades of experience in SEO, branding, and performance marketing, he serves as Lead Strategist at a nationally recognized digital agency and CMO of a leading media network. His work empowers entrepreneurs and enterprise leaders to **stand out in crowded markets**, build lasting authority, and grow with confidence in a fast-changing digital world.